Pebble Plus

Exploring the Galaxy
Neptune

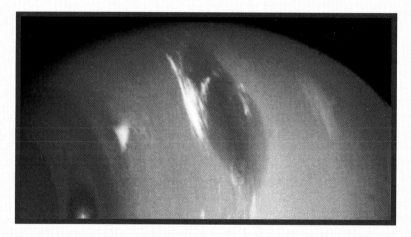

by Thomas K. Adamson

Consulting Editor: Gail Saunders-Smith, Ph.D.

Consultant: James Gerard
Aerospace Education Specialist, NASA
Kennedy Space Center, Florida

Pebble Plus is published by Capstone Press
151 Good Counsel Drive, P.O. Box 669, Mankato, Minnesota 56002
http://www.capstone-press.com

1 2 3 4 5 6 08 07 06 05 04 03

Library of Congress Cataloging-in-Publication Data
Adamson, Thomas K., 1970–
    Neptune / by Thomas K. Adamson.
    p. cm.—(Pebble Plus: exploring the galaxy)
    Summary: Simple text and photographs describe the planet Neptune.
    Includes bibliographical references and index.
    ISBN 0-7368-2115-5 (hardcover)
    1. Neptune (Planet)—Juvenile literature. [1. Neptune (Planet)] I. Title. II. Series.
QB691 .A33 2004
523.48′1—dc21   2002155604

Editorial Credits
Mari C. Schuh, editor; Kia Adams, designer; Alta Schaffer, photo researcher; Eric Kudalis, product planning editor

Photo Credits
Digital Vision, 5 (Venus)
NASA, 1, 4 (Pluto), 7, 15, 17, 21; JPL, 5 (Jupiter); JPL/Caltech, 5 (Uranus), 13
PhotoDisc Inc., cover, 4 (Neptune), 5 (Mars, Mercury, Earth, Sun, Saturn), 11 (both); Stock Trek, 9, 19

Note to Parents and Teachers

The Exploring the Galaxy series supports national science standards related to earth science. This book describes and illustrates the planet Neptune. The photographs support early readers in understanding the text. The repetition of words and phrases helps early readers learn new words. This book also introduces early readers to subject-specific vocabulary words, which are defined in the Glossary section. Early readers may need assistance to read some words and to use the Table of Contents, Glossary, Read More, Internet Sites, and Index/Word List sections of the book.

Word Count: 124
Early-Intervention Level: 14

Table of Contents

Neptune

Neptune is the eighth planet from the Sun. Neptune looks bright blue.

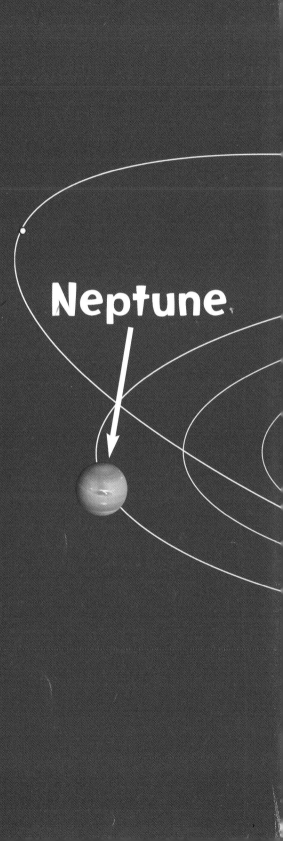

Neptune

The Solar System

Sun

Clouds

Neptune is a big ball
of gases and clouds.
It is called a gas giant.

7

White clouds move across
Neptune. The clouds often
change shape.

9

Neptune's Size

Neptune is the fourth largest planet. Neptune is almost four times wider than Earth.

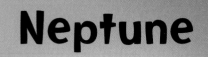

Neptune

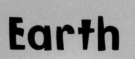

Earth

11

Neptune's Moons

At least 11 moons move around Neptune. Most of the moons are small, icy chunks of rock.

Neptune's largest moon is called Triton. It is made of rock and ice.

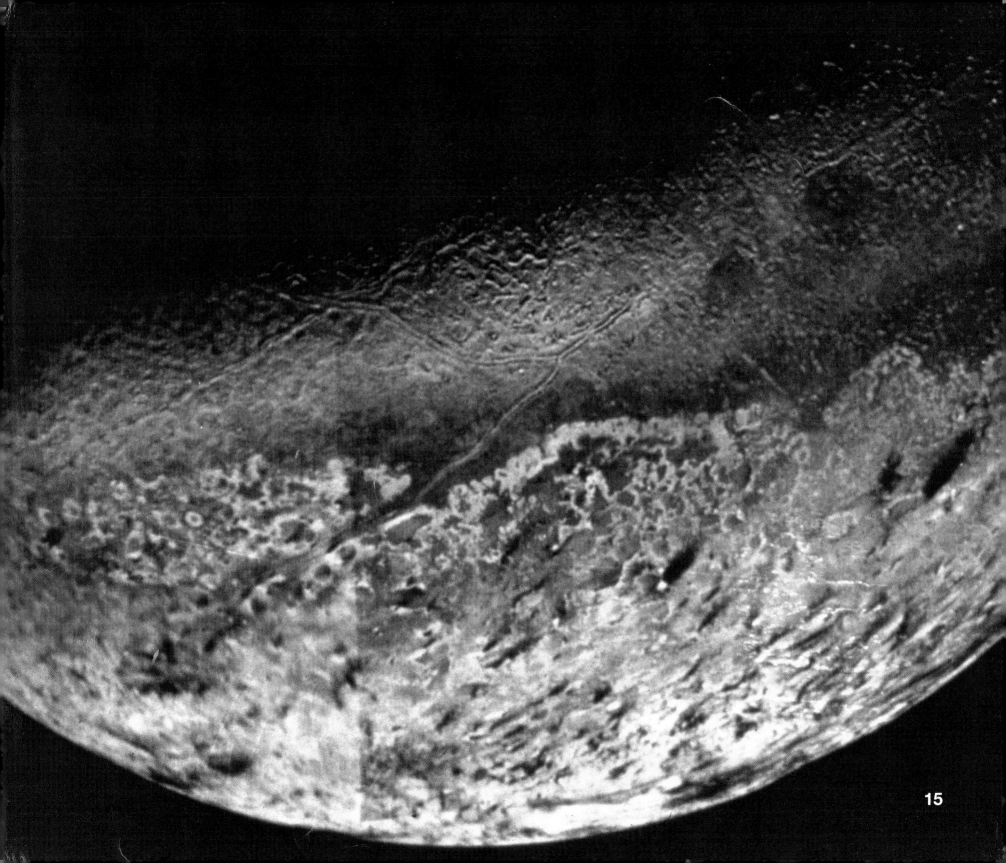

15

Triton probably looks like the planet Pluto. Triton is one of the coldest places in the solar system.

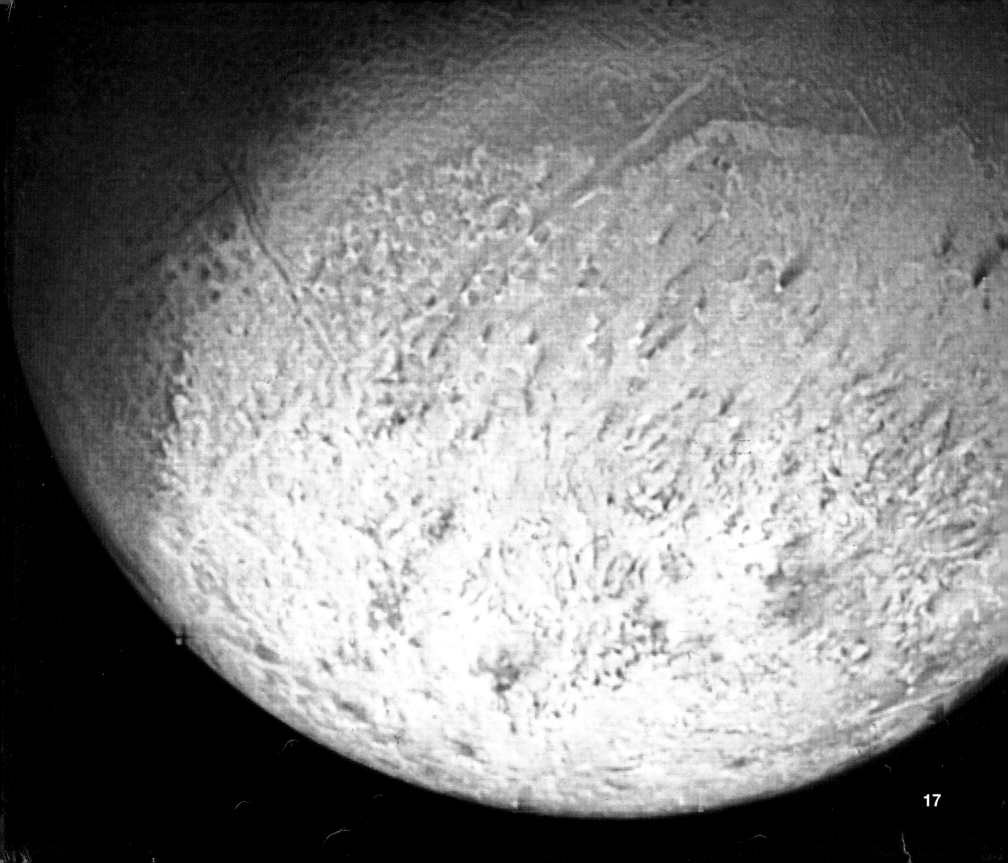

17

People and Neptune

Neptune does not have
a solid surface. People
could not live on Neptune.

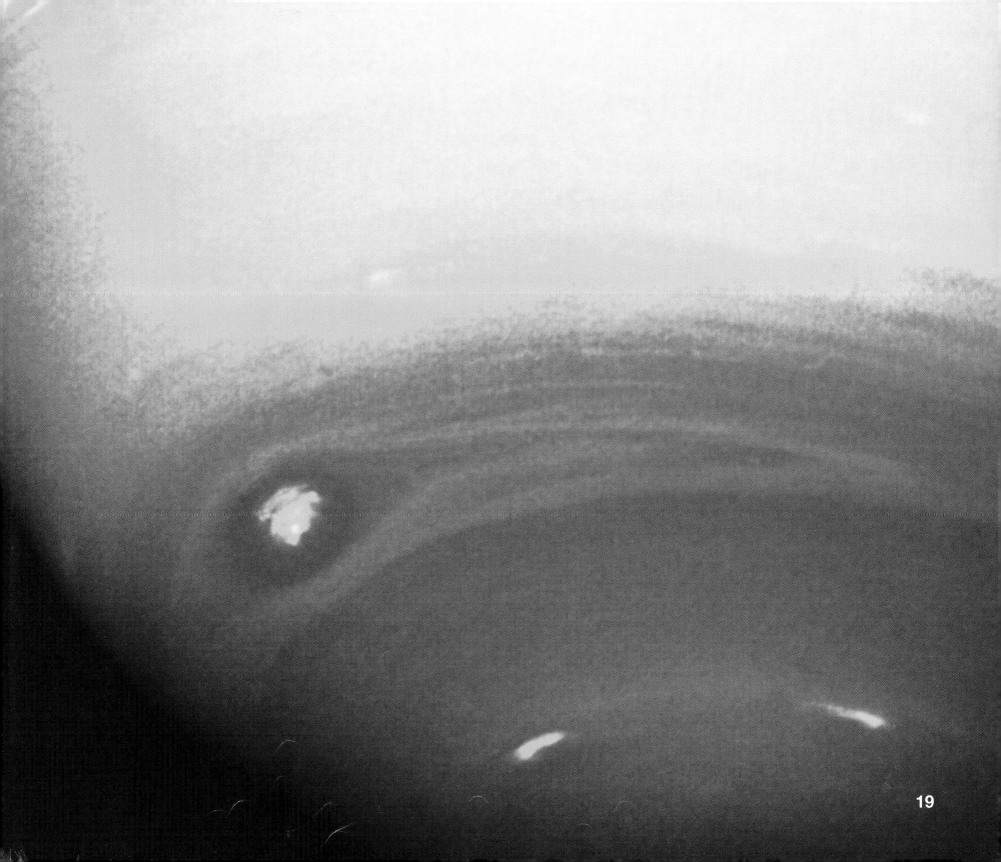

People cannot see Neptune
without a telescope. Neptune
is too far away.

Glossary

gas—a substance, such as air, that spreads to fill any space that holds it; Neptune is called a gas giant; the other gas giants are Jupiter, Saturn, and Uranus.

moon—an object that moves around a planet

planet—a large object that moves around the Sun; Neptune is the eighth planet from the Sun.

Sun—the star that the planets move around; the Sun provides light and heat for the planets.

telescope—a tool people use to look at planets and other objects in space; telescopes make planets and other objects look closer than they really are.

Read More

Goss, Tim. *Uranus, Neptune, and Pluto.* The Universe. Chicago: Heinemann Library, 2003.

Miller, Ron. *Uranus and Neptune.* Worlds Beyond. Brookfield, Conn.: Twenty-First Century Books, 2003.

Thompson, Luke. *Neptune.* The Library of the Planets. New York: PowerKids Press, 2001.

Vogt, Gregory. *Neptune.* The Galaxy. Mankato, Minn.: Bridgestone Books, 2000.

Internet Sites

Do you want to find out more about Neptune and the solar system? Let FactHound, our fact-finding hound dog, do the research for you.

Here's how:

1) Visit *http://www.facthound.com*

2) Type in the **Book ID** number: **0736821155**

3) Click on **FETCH IT**.

FactHound will fetch Internet sites picked by our editors just for you!

Index/Word List